The Tullock – Padgett Family Of Delano

David Russell Tullock

The Tullock – Padgett Family of Delano

Copyright © 2014 by David Russell Tullock

This book was printed in the United States of America.

To order additional copies of this book, contact:

Parson's Porch & Company

1-423-475-7308

www.parsonsporch.com

Tulloch

Pedigree Chart for
James Russell Tullock

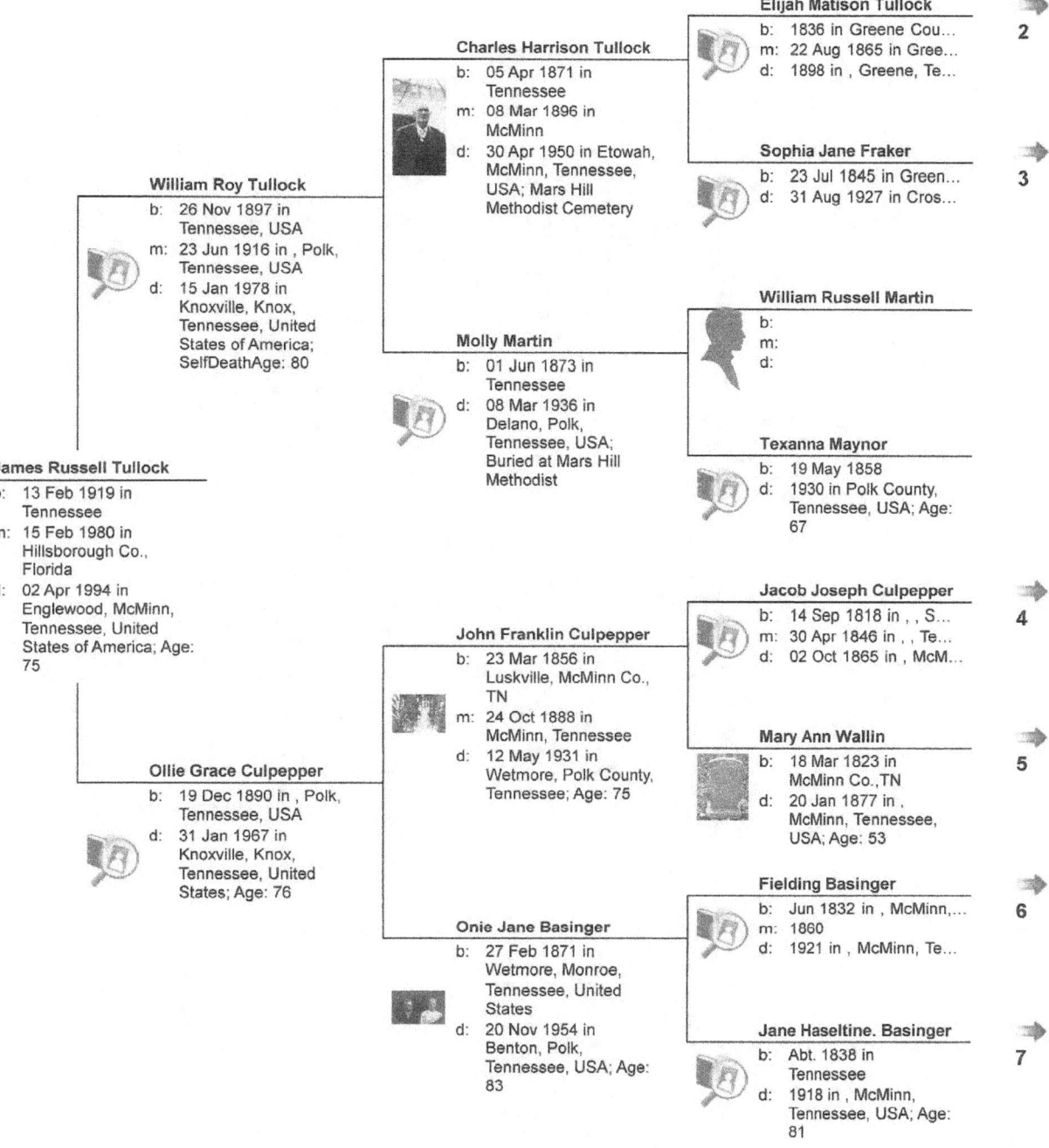

James Russell Tullock
b: 13 Feb 1919 in Tennessee
m: 15 Feb 1980 in Hillsborough Co., Florida
d: 02 Apr 1994 in Englewood, McMinn, Tennessee, United States of America; Age: 75

William Roy Tullock
b: 26 Nov 1897 in Tennessee, USA
m: 23 Jun 1916 in , Polk, Tennessee, USA
d: 15 Jan 1978 in Knoxville, Knox, Tennessee, United States of America; SelfDeathAge: 80

Charles Harrison Tullock
b: 05 Apr 1871 in Tennessee
m: 08 Mar 1896 in McMinn
d: 30 Apr 1950 in Etowah, McMinn, Tennessee, USA; Mars Hill Methodist Cemetery

Elijah Matison Tullock
b: 1836 in Greene Cou...
m: 22 Aug 1865 in Gree...
d: 1898 in , Greene, Te...
2

Sophia Jane Fraker
b: 23 Jul 1845 in Green...
d: 31 Aug 1927 in Cros...
3

Molly Martin
b: 01 Jun 1873 in Tennessee
d: 08 Mar 1936 in Delano, Polk, Tennessee, USA; Buried at Mars Hill Methodist

William Russell Martin
b:
m:
d:

Texanna Maynor
b: 19 May 1858
d: 1930 in Polk County, Tennessee, USA; Age: 67

Ollie Grace Culpepper
b: 19 Dec 1890 in , Polk, Tennessee, USA
d: 31 Jan 1967 in Knoxville, Knox, Tennessee, United States; Age: 76

John Franklin Culpepper
b: 23 Mar 1856 in Luskville, McMinn Co., TN
m: 24 Oct 1888 in McMinn, Tennessee
d: 12 May 1931 in Wetmore, Polk County, Tennessee; Age: 75

Jacob Joseph Culpepper
b: 14 Sep 1818 in , , S...
m: 30 Apr 1846 in , , Te...
d: 02 Oct 1865 in , McM...
4

Mary Ann Wallin
b: 18 Mar 1823 in McMinn Co.,TN
d: 20 Jan 1877 in , McMinn, Tennessee, USA; Age: 53
5

Onie Jane Basinger
b: 27 Feb 1871 in Wetmore, Monroe, Tennessee, United States
d: 20 Nov 1954 in Benton, Polk, Tennessee, USA; Age: 83

Fielding Basinger
b: Jun 1832 in , McMinn,...
m: 1860
d: 1921 in , McMinn, Te...
6

Jane Haseltine. Basinger
b: Abt. 1838 in Tennessee
d: 1918 in , McMinn, Tennessee, USA; Age: 81
7

Adam Fraker

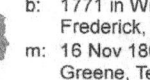

- b: 1771 in Winchester, Frederick, Virginia, USA
- m: 16 Nov 1803 in , Greene, Tennessee, USA
- d: 1860 in , Greene, Tennessee, USA

Frederick Fraker

- b: 1805 in , Greene, Tennessee, USA
- m: 26 Jun 1840 in Greene County,TN
- d: 1880 in Greene, Tennessee, United States

Elizabeth Loyd

- b: 09 Apr 1786 in Pennsylvania, Lancaster, Pennsylvania, USA
- d: 1860 in Tiffin, Seneca, Ohio, USA

Sophia Jane Fraker

- b: 23 Jul 1845 in Greenville, Greene, Tennessee, United States
- m: 22 Aug 1865 in Greene, Tennessee
- d: 31 Aug 1927 in Cross Anchor Cemeter, Green Co., Tennessee; Age: 82

1

Uriah Collins

- b: 01 Mar 1778 in VA
- m: Apr 1806
- d: 04 Jan 1864 in Greeneville, Greene, TN

Betsy Collins

- b: 28 Oct 1811 in Greene, Tennessee, United States
- d: 1880 in Greene, Tennessee, United States

Elizabeth Sellars

- b: Abt. 1794 in VA
- d: Abt. 1860 in Greene, TN

Lewis Brewer

b: 1760 in Exeter,
Devon, England

m: 1787 in Elk Creek,
Grayson, Virginia,
United States

d: 07 Mar 1839 in Elk
Creek, Grayson,
Virginia, USA

Lewis Brewer

b: 12 Oct 1795 in Elk
Creek, Grayson,
Virginia, United States

m: 09 Mar 1820 in
Grayson, Virginia

d: 04 Dec 1856 in
McMinn, Tennessee,
United States

Agatha Holland

b: 10 May 1768 in
Austinville, Wythe,
Virginia, United States

d: 21 Nov 1862 in Elk
Creek, Grayson,
Virginia, United States

Jane Haseltine. Basinger

b: Abt. 1838 in
Tennessee

m: 1860

d: 1918 in , McMinn,
Tennessee, USA; Age:
81

Name:

b:

m:

d:

1

Susanna Poole Bedwell

b: 1800 in Elk Creek,
Grayson, Virginia,
United States

d: 1825 in Greene,
Indiana, United States

Name:

b:

d:

James Russell Tullock
and Eunice Lola Padgett

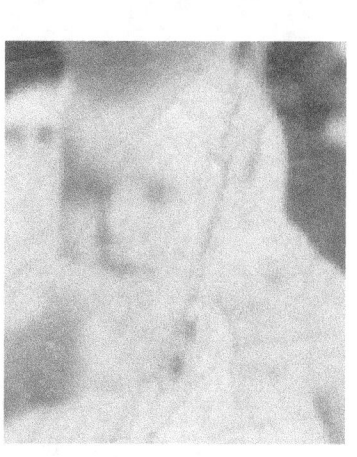

Bob

Patsy

Linda

Alfred

Becki

James Robert Tullock

School Days
1946-47

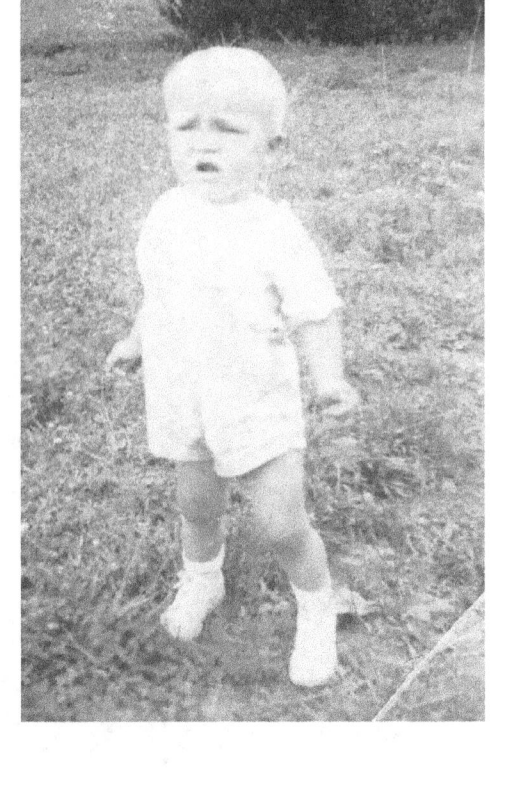

Patsy Dean Tullock

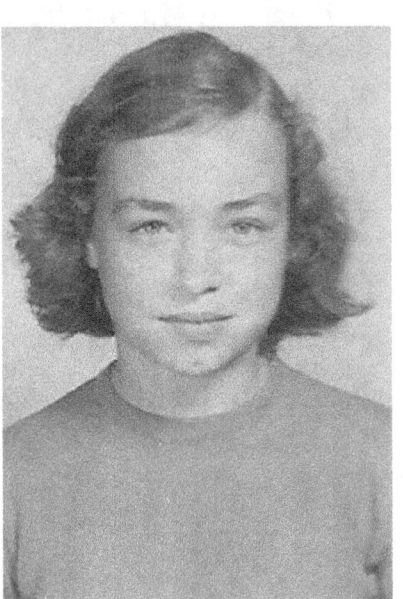

Hoyt Knox

Rex Tipton

Jim Wilson

Gene Loudermilk

Alfred Leon Tullock

Rebecca Diane Tullock

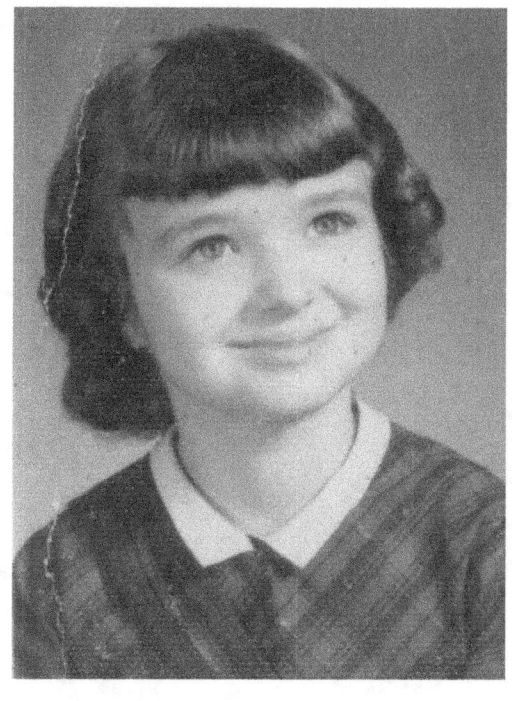

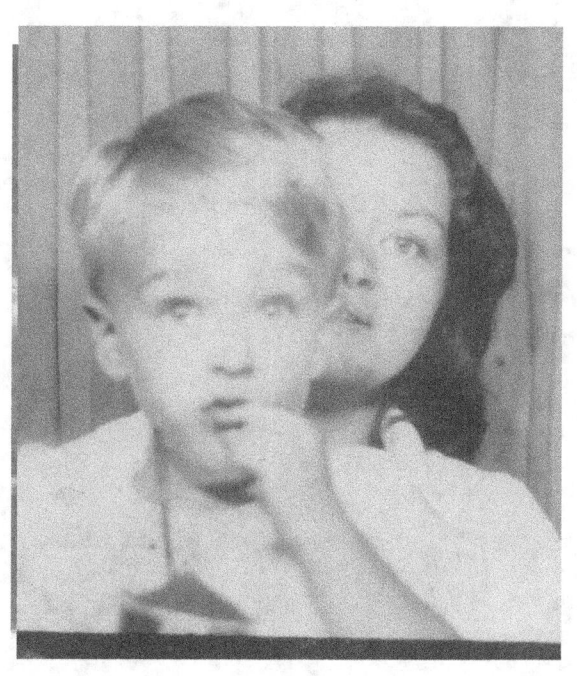

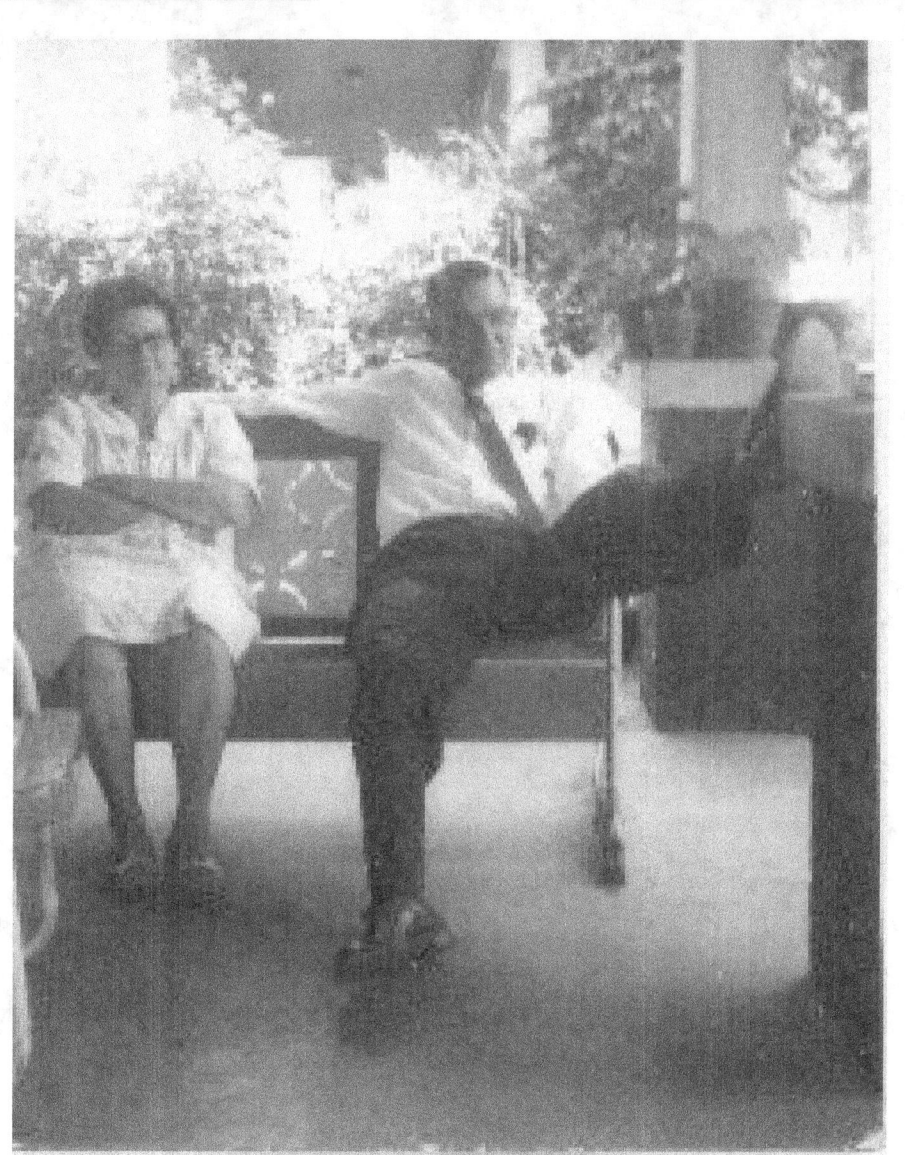

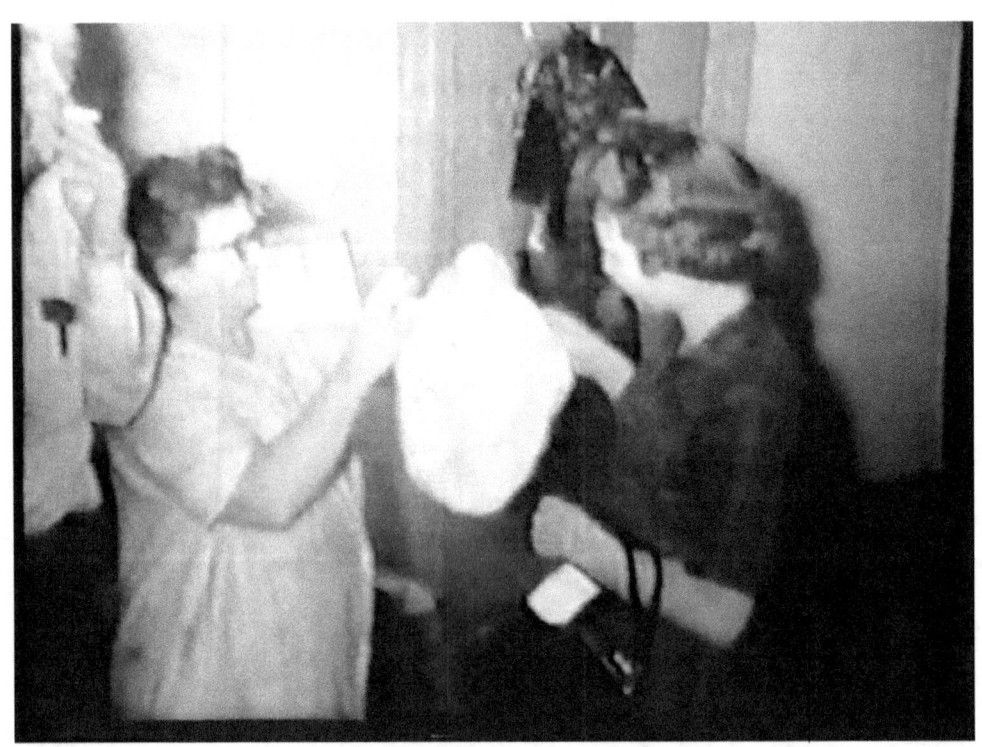

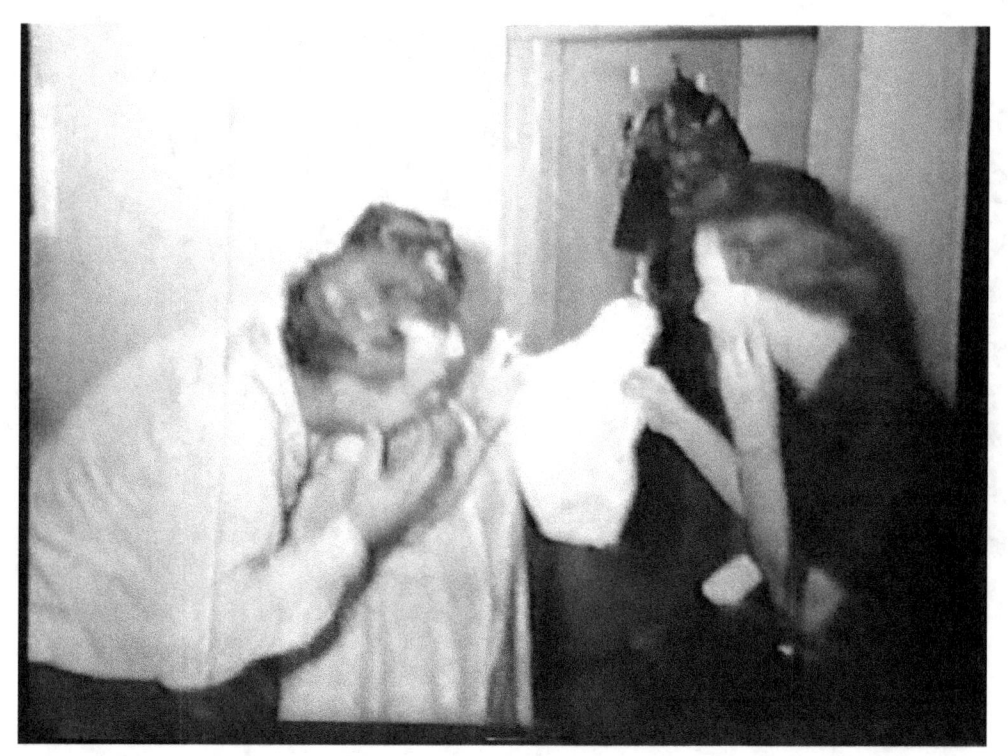

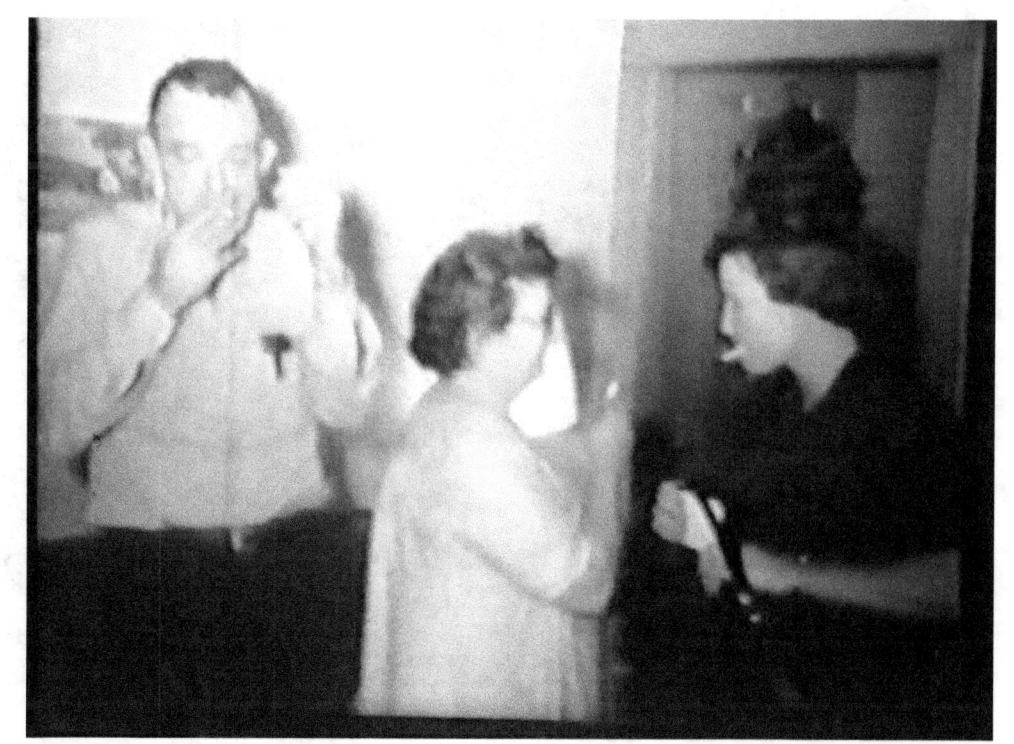

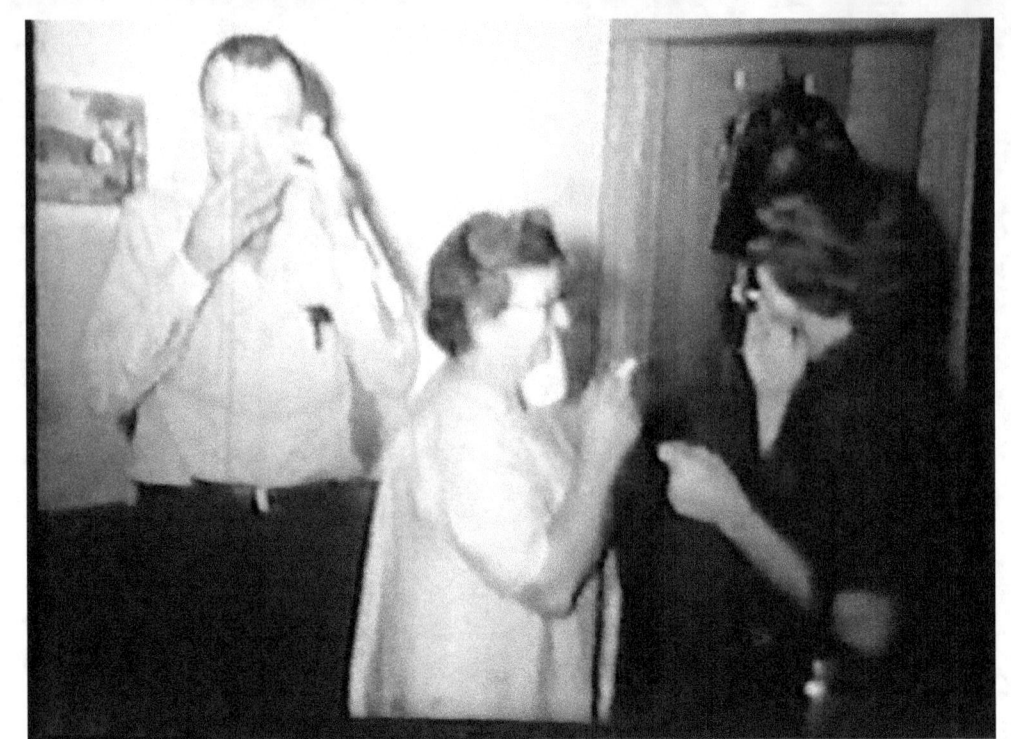

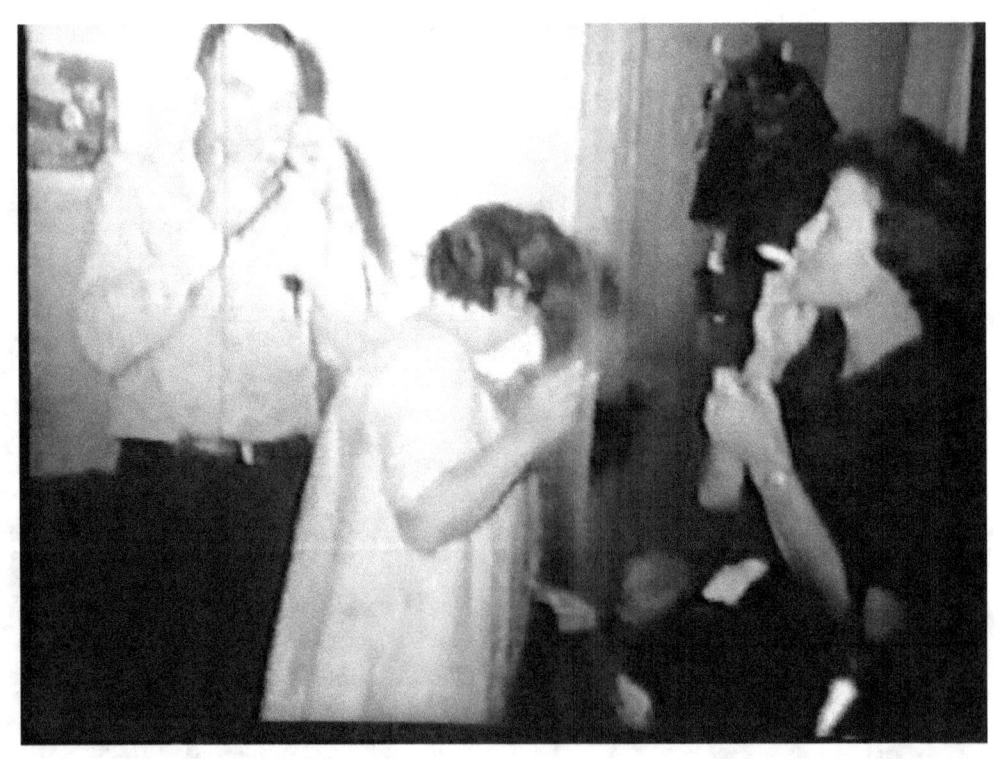

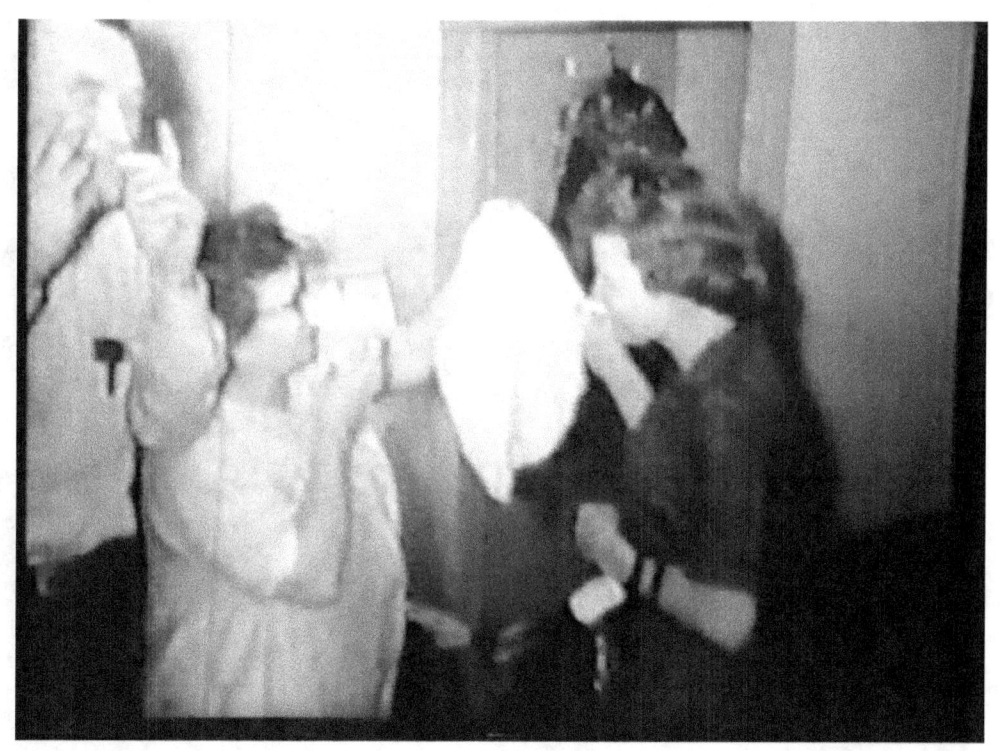

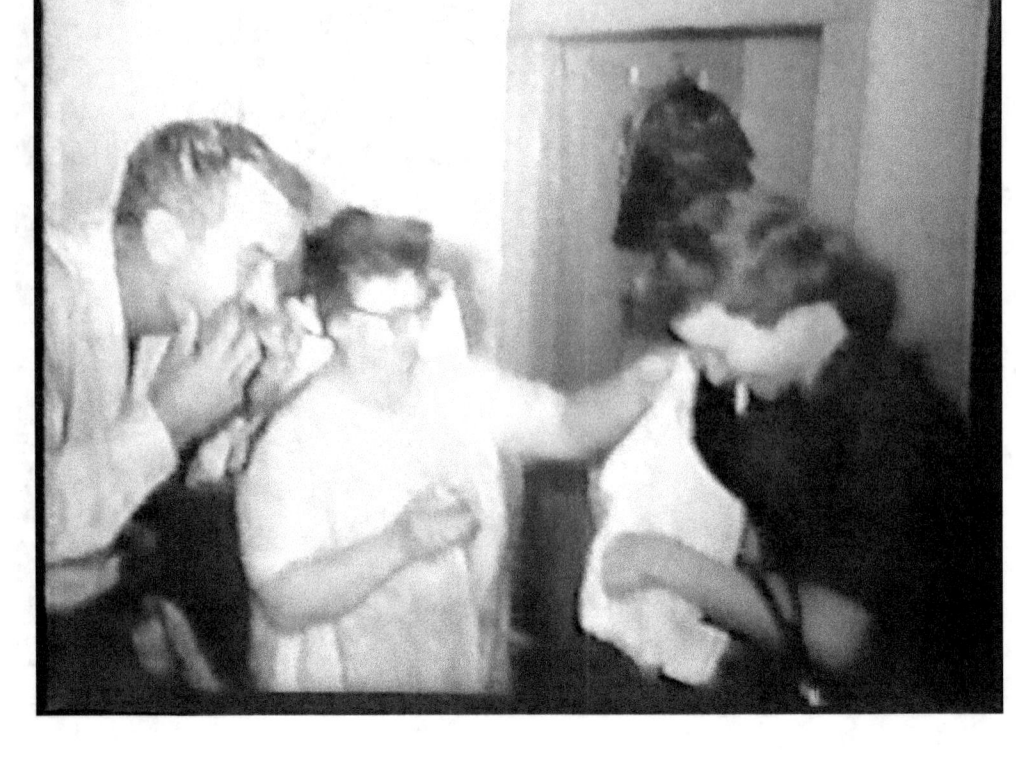

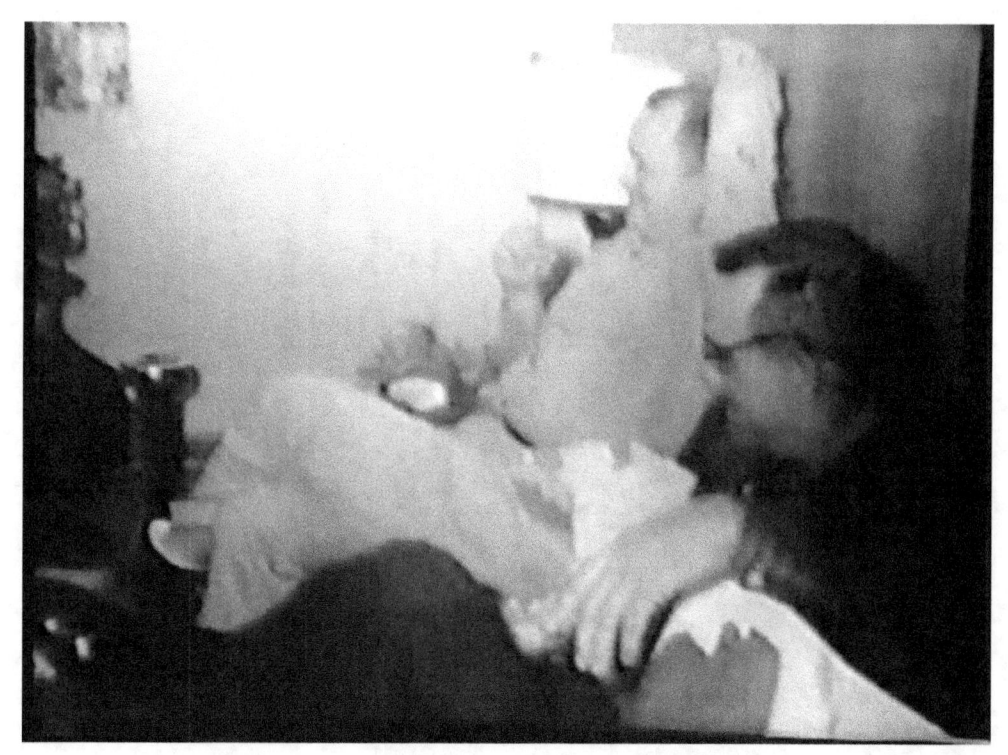

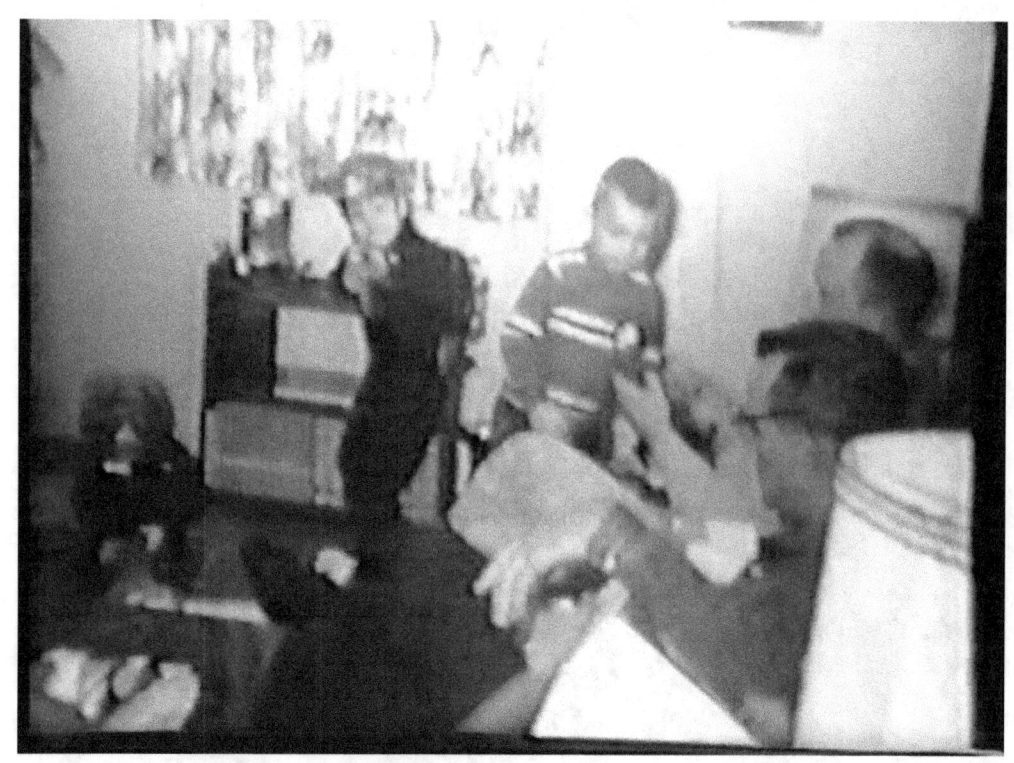

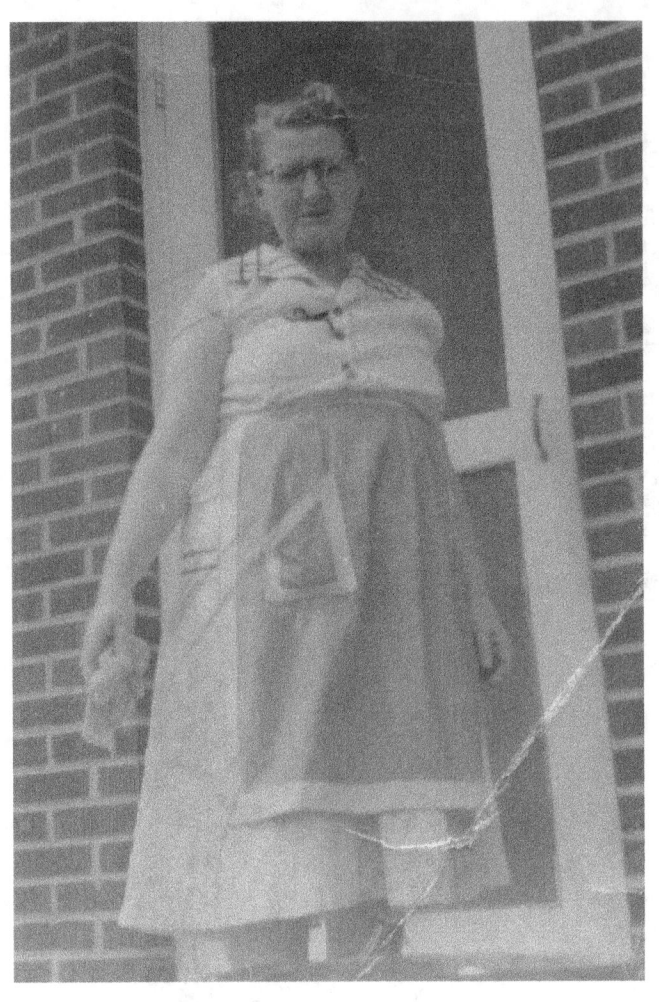

Elijah Matison Tullock and Sophia Fraker

Charles Harrison   James Chadwick   Julie

Eunice   Zackary Taylor   William Duke

James Chadwick Tullock

English Pierce

Lura

Samuel

English Pierce Tullock

Billie Lou Tullock

School Days
1941-42

English Pierce (Jake) Tullock, Jr.

Aileen Tullock

Lillian Tullock

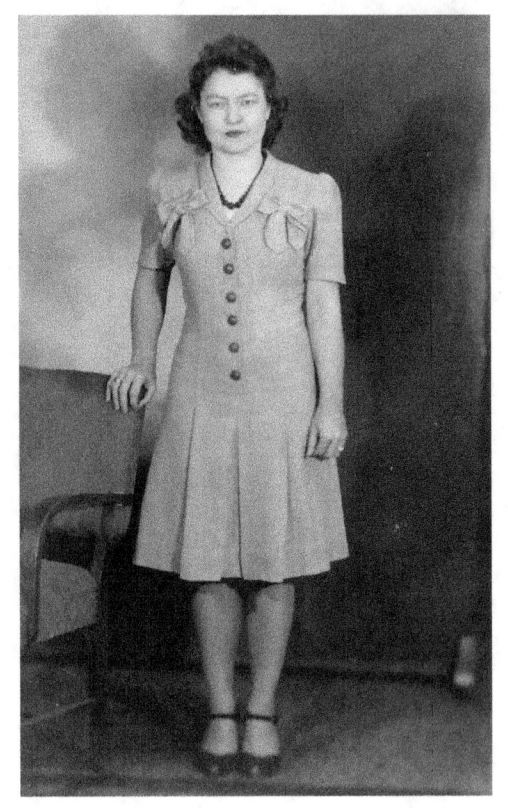

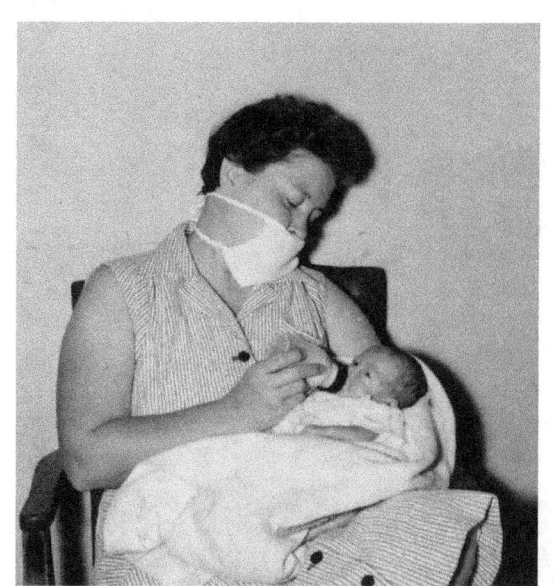

Doug Tullock

SCHOOL DAYS 1952-53
ETOWAH

Lura Tullock

Sam Tullock and Carrie Visage

Zachary Taylor Tullock

Julie Tullock's Daughter

Charles Harrison Tullock and Mary Quinton

Robert C. Tullock

Thomas Tullock

Robert C. Tullock and Hattie Griggs

Hattie Tullock's marker

Josephine standing at Grandpa Tullocks grave

Geneva and George Horton

Ralph and Mary

Ralph & kids   Steven   Joyce   Sonny   Jack standing

Charles Harrison Tullock and Molly Martin

William Roy   Nellie   Rhoda

Sophia   Paul   Maude

Rhoda   Sophia Charlie Nellie Maude   Roy

Roy Tullock's Birthplace - Old Athens Rd.

William Roy Tullock
and Ollie Grace Culpepper

Hubert   Willie   Flossy   James

Jane   Jody   Jack   John

Lois   Betty

William Roy and Hazel

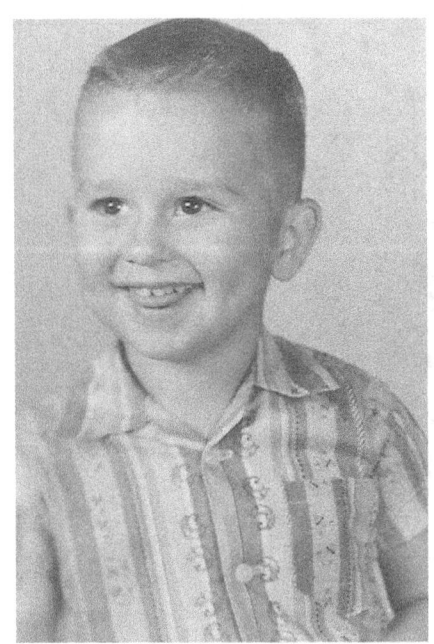 

Leroy Henderson   Jimmy Henderson

Back — Willie and Buck Front — James, Flossy and Jack

Flossy and James

Hubert "Buck" Sartain and Edith

Willie Roberta Sartain and Clarence Burris

Seasons Greetings

Herbert C. Ritchie and Family

Flossie Evelyn Tullock and James McClain

James Russell Tullock and Eunice Padgett

Jack Wilson Tullock and Helen Lee

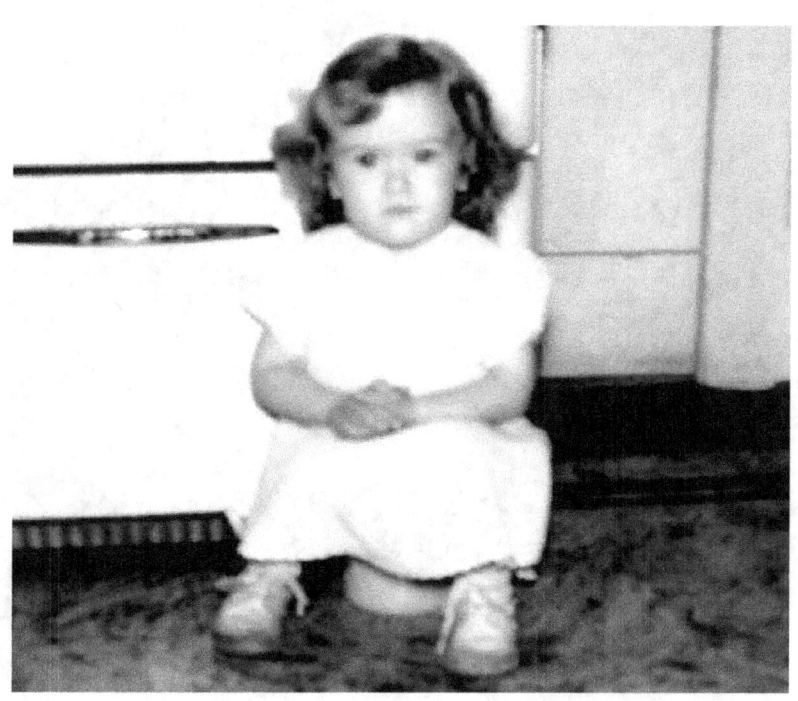

Mildred Jane Tullock and Alfred Newman

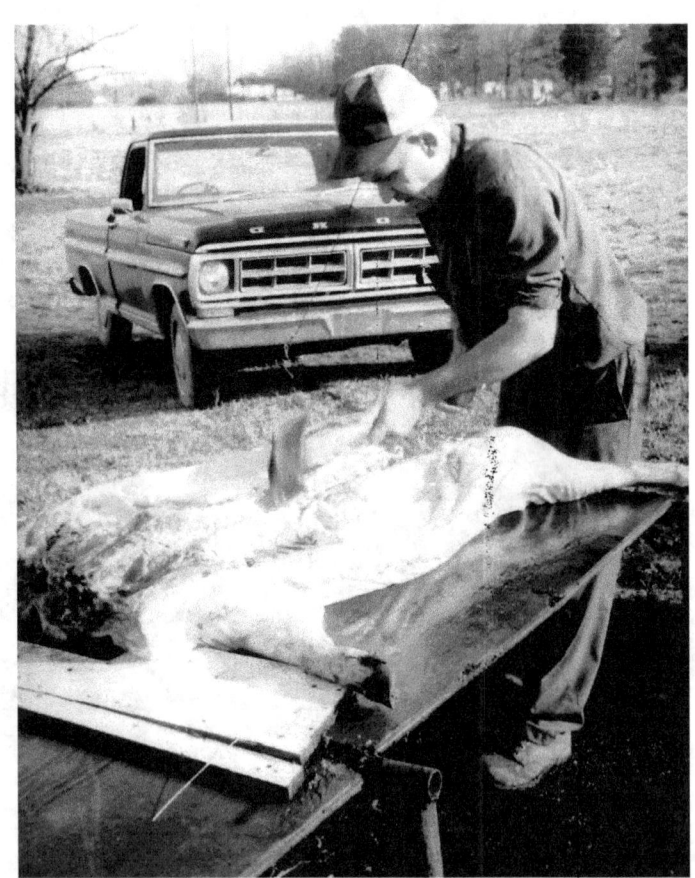

William Roy "Jody" Tullock and Helen Claiborne

Virginia Lois Tullock and Clyde Miller

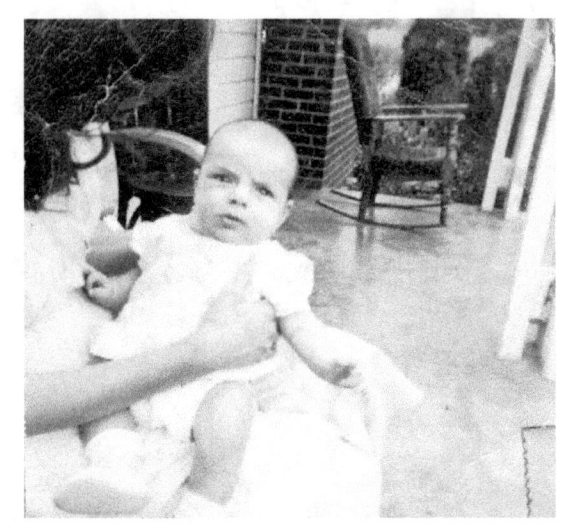

John Harrison Tullock and Helen Curtis

Betty Tullock and C.H. Sterling

MRS. C. H. STERLING, JR.

52   Betty Tullock

Sophia Tullock and Sam (Red) Magness

Lolita Magness

Juanita Magness

Rhoda Tullock and Kenneth Thacker

Maude Tullock and Raymond Stokes

Nellie Tullock and Arlie Newman

Paul Tullock and Estelle

William Dyke Tullock

Fielding Pope Basinger and Betsy Brewer

John Franklin Culpepper and Onie Basinger

Malcolm

John Harold
(Socky)

Millie

Charles

Ed

Robert Hugh
Culpepper
-Jimmy-

1. Leslie (Pes)
2. Mellie
3. Eunice
4. Paul
5. Mauda
6. Pete
7. Ollie
8. Ed
9. Dolph
10. Grandmother
11. Malcolm
12. Harold (Sacky)
13. Norman (Babe)
14. Charles - not pictured
15. Robert   "   "
16. Dora - deceased
17. Evans   "
18. Grafton   "
19. Joe - not pictured.

767 The Culpeppers

Wetmore Baptish Church 1928

Charles Culpepper

Ed Culpepper

Joe and Essie Culpepper

Mellie Culpepper

Paul Culpepper

"Cotton"
Pete's
boy

Bill
Culpepper

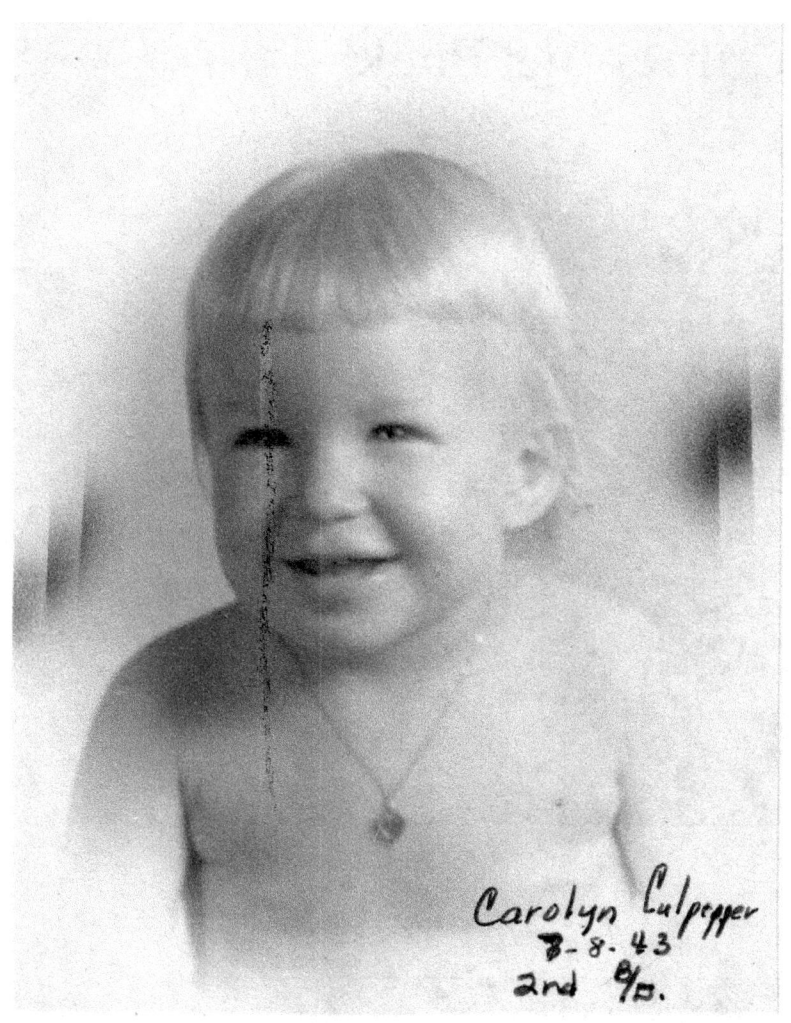

Carolyn Culpepper
8-8-43
2nd 8/D.

Amos Culpepper - Leslie's son

Maude Culpepper Pack

Maude Culpepper and her daughter Jean Pack

Jean Pack and her daughter Charlene

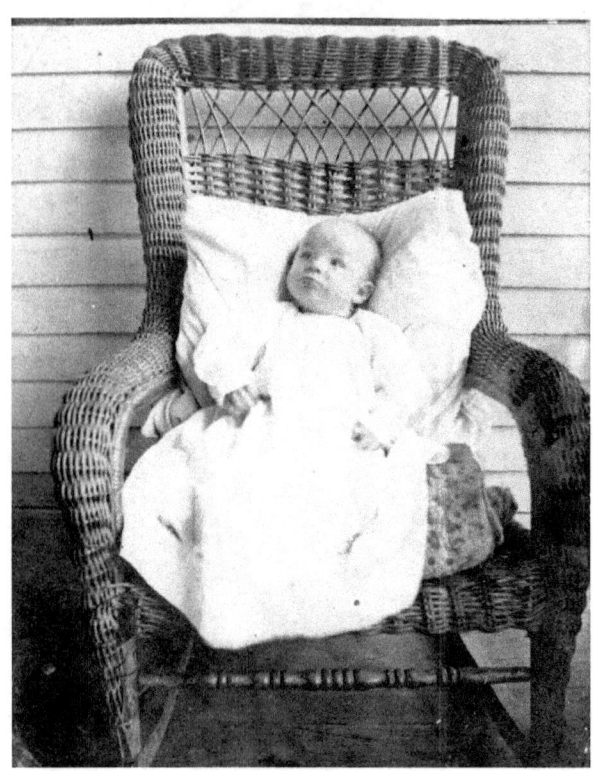

Helen C. Kennedy + husband

Leon

Padgett

Pedigree Chart for
Eunice Lola Padgett

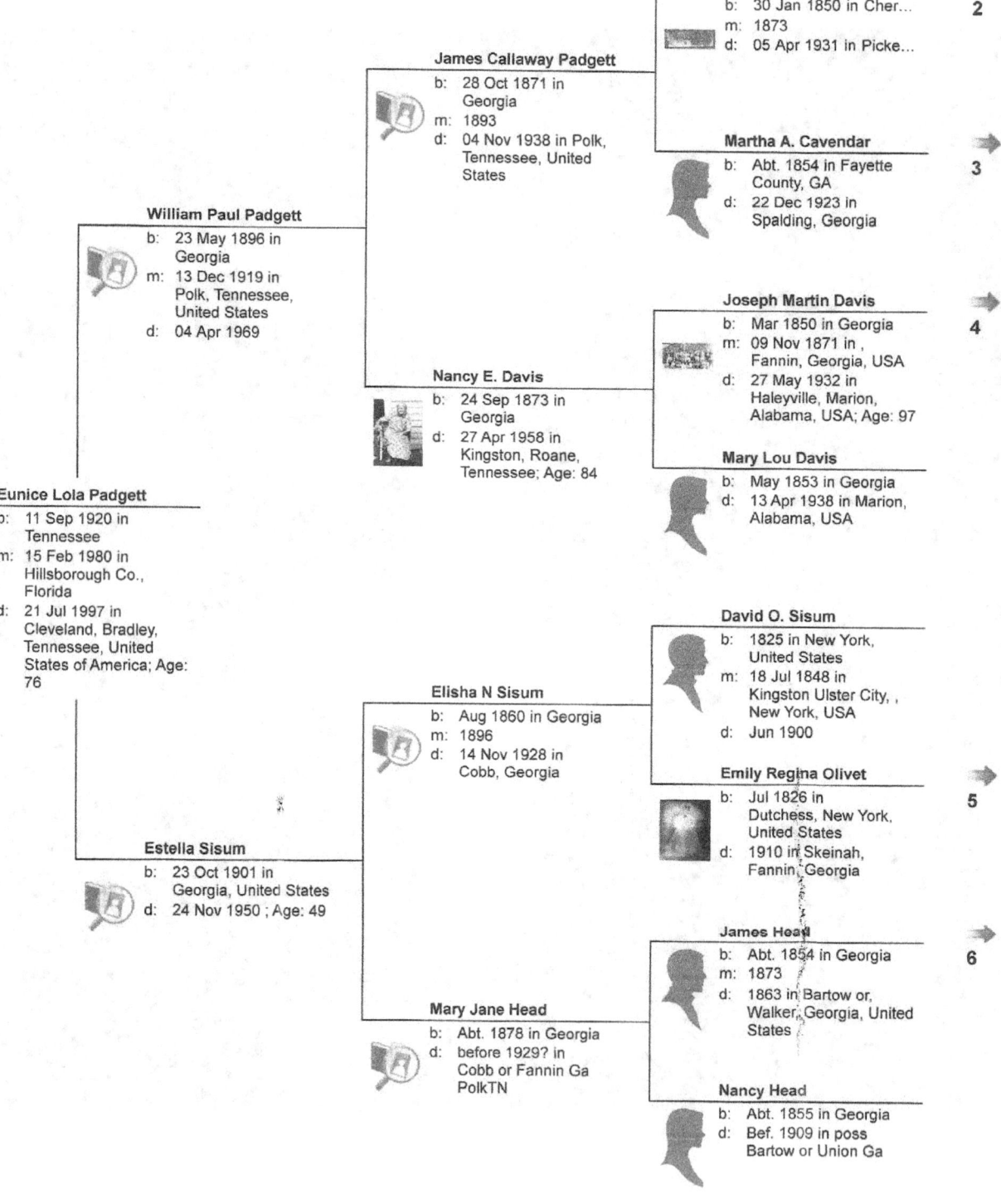

Elisha C Padgett
b: 30 Jan 1850 in Cher...
m: 1873
d: 05 Apr 1931 in Picke...
→ 2

James Callaway Padgett
b: 28 Oct 1871 in Georgia
m: 1893
d: 04 Nov 1938 in Polk, Tennessee, United States

Martha A. Cavendar
b: Abt. 1854 in Fayette County, GA
d: 22 Dec 1923 in Spalding, Georgia
→ 3

William Paul Padgett
b: 23 May 1896 in Georgia
m: 13 Dec 1919 in Polk, Tennessee, United States
d: 04 Apr 1969

Joseph Martin Davis
b: Mar 1850 in Georgia
m: 09 Nov 1871 in , Fannin, Georgia, USA
d: 27 May 1932 in Haleyville, Marion, Alabama, USA; Age: 97
→ 4

Nancy E. Davis
b: 24 Sep 1873 in Georgia
d: 27 Apr 1958 in Kingston, Roane, Tennessee; Age: 84

Mary Lou Davis
b: May 1853 in Georgia
d: 13 Apr 1938 in Marion, Alabama, USA

Eunice Lola Padgett
b: 11 Sep 1920 in Tennessee
m: 15 Feb 1980 in Hillsborough Co., Florida
d: 21 Jul 1997 in Cleveland, Bradley, Tennessee, United States of America; Age: 76

David O. Sisum
b: 1825 in New York, United States
m: 18 Jul 1848 in Kingston Ulster City, , New York, USA
d: Jun 1900

Elisha N Sisum
b: Aug 1860 in Georgia
m: 1896
d: 14 Nov 1928 in Cobb, Georgia

Emily Regina Olivet
b: Jul 1826 in Dutchess, New York, United States
d: 1910 in Skeinah, Fannin, Georgia
→ 5

Estella Sisum
b: 23 Oct 1901 in Georgia, United States
d: 24 Nov 1950 ; Age: 49

James Head
b: Abt. 1854 in Georgia
m: 1873
d: 1863 in Bartow or, Walker, Georgia, United States
→ 6

Mary Jane Head
b: Abt. 1878 in Georgia
d: before 1929? in Cobb or Fannin Ga PolkTN

Nancy Head
b: Abt. 1855 in Georgia
d: Bef. 1909 in poss Bartow or Union Ga

Rev Jesse Padgett
b: 18 Jun 1802 in

Joseph Cavender

- b: 1766 in Westmoreland County, Virginia
- m: 1810 in Pendleton, Anderson, South Carolina
- d: 1858 in Maury, Tennessee, USA

Wade Hampton Cavender

- b: 1817 in , , Georgia, USA
- m: 13 Feb 1840 in , Fayette, Georgia, USA
- d: 10 May 1847 in Tyrone, Fayette, Georgia, USA

Miriam Henry

- b: 1789 in North Carolina
- d: 1836 in Walker County, Georgia

Martha A. Cavendar

- b: Abt. 1854 in Fayette County, GA
- m: 1873
- d: 22 Dec 1923 in Spalding, Georgia

1

William James Brasselle

- b: 24 Mar 1778 in North Carolina, United States
- m: 31 Oct 1809 in North Carolina, United States
- d: 16 Jun 1861 in Fayette, Georgia, United States

Delilah Brassell

- b: 20 Jul 1816 in , Fayette, Georgia, USA
- d: 1900 in , Fayette, Georgia, USA

Martha Haddox

- b: 07 Apr 1795 in Edgefield, Edgefield, South Carolina, United States
- d: 13 Mar 1836 in Fayette, Georgia, United States

Name:
b:
m:
d:

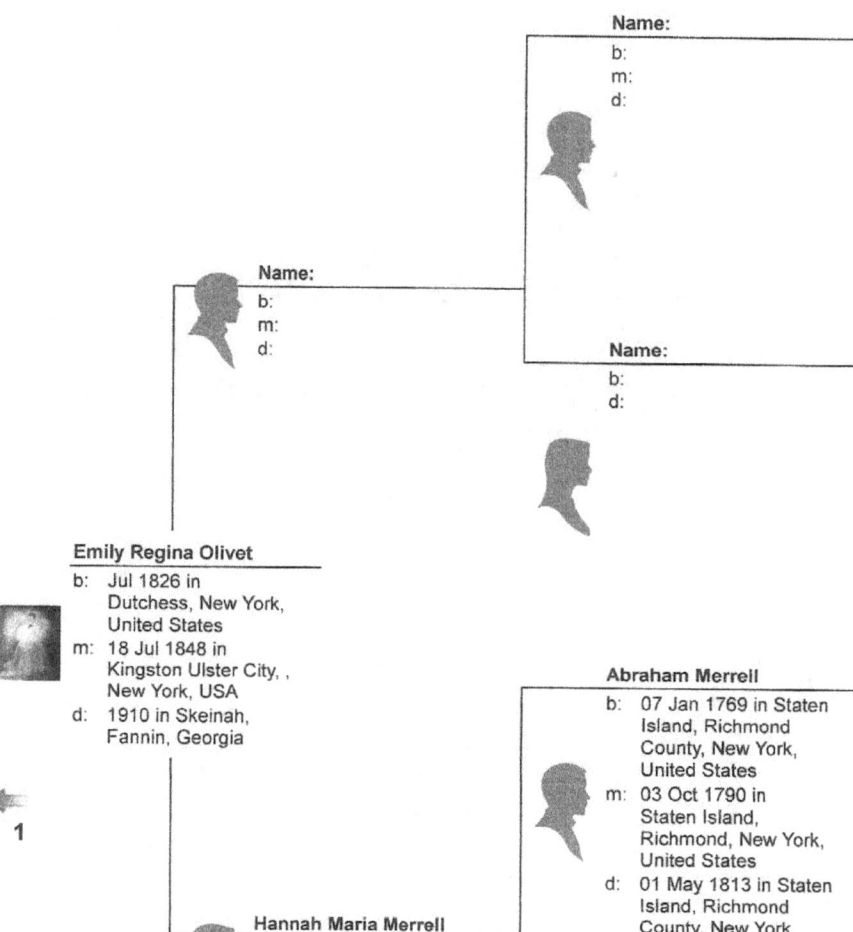

Name:
b:
m:
d:

Name:
b:
d:

Emily Regina Olivet

b: Jul 1826 in
Dutchess, New York,
United States
m: 18 Jul 1848 in
Kingston Ulster City, ,
New York, USA
d: 1910 in Skeinah,
Fannin, Georgia

1

Abraham Merrell

b: 07 Jan 1769 in Staten
Island, Richmond
County, New York,
United States
m: 03 Oct 1790 in
Staten Island,
Richmond, New York,
United States
d: 01 May 1813 in Staten
Island, Richmond
County, New York

Hannah Maria Merrell

b: 1805 in NY
d: 02 Aug 1849 in
Flatbush, Queens, New
York, United States

Annie Merrell

b: 20 Feb 1774 in Staten
Island, Richmond
County, New York

 d:

Jesse and Edy Padgett

Eunice's 4th great grandfather

John C. – Pony - Padget and Sarah Deniza

Eunice's 3rd great grandfather and grandmother

Corinth Baptist Church

Padget Clan

The Padgett

Back Row
Pa Padgett, Barney Adams, Homer Padgett
Sign Padgett, Riley Padgett, Dick Padgett, Venie Hogan
Mamie Padgett, Bessie Padgett, Sarah Reed, Nano R
Martha Padgett, Febbie Worly, Denizo Padgett,
Charley Padgett, Elizabeth Padgett, Willie Hogan.

Millard Padgett, Pack Adams, Andrew Padgett
Allen Cantrell (sister girl) John Adams, Daneil Padgett
Ponnie and Granny Padgett, Turner Padgett
Cosie Lee Hogan.

Hix Jones Wray

Nancy Davis Padgett's Grandfather

Elizabeth Davis Wray

Joseph Martin Davis

Nancy Davis Padgett

James Callaway Padgett and Nancy Davis

Carl

Roy

Paul

Jane

Mary

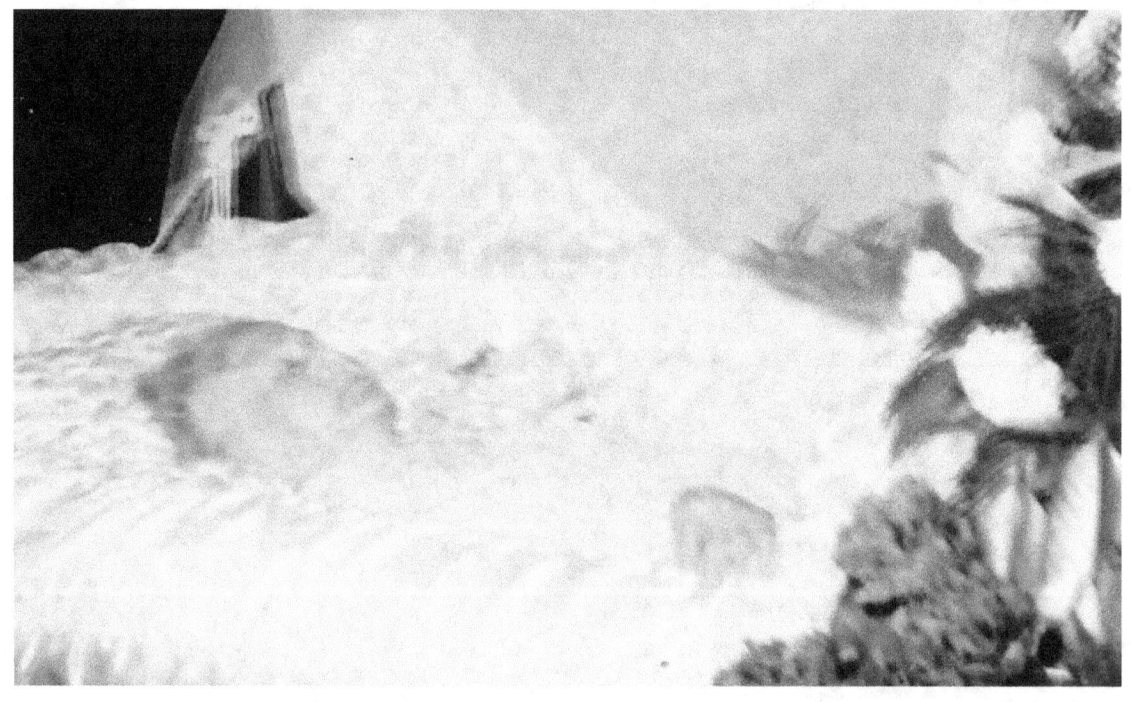

Arlin Padgett

James C. Padgett's Brother

Paul Padgett and Estelle Sisum

Eunice Lola

John Edward

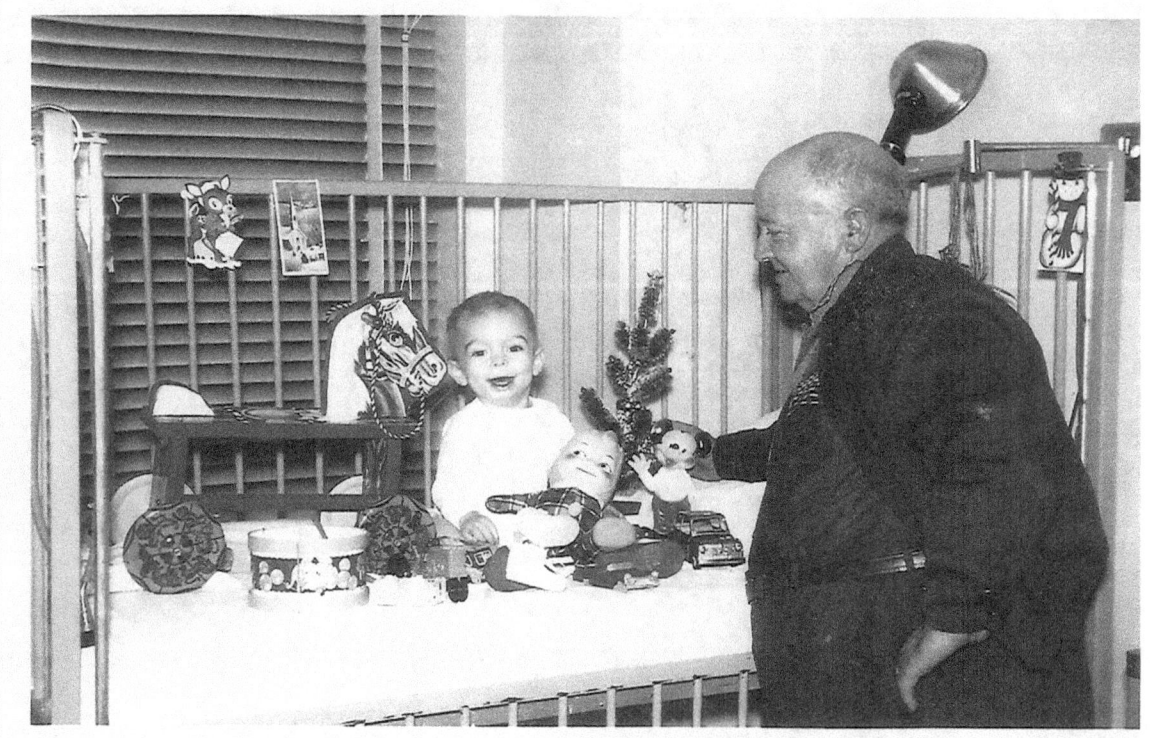

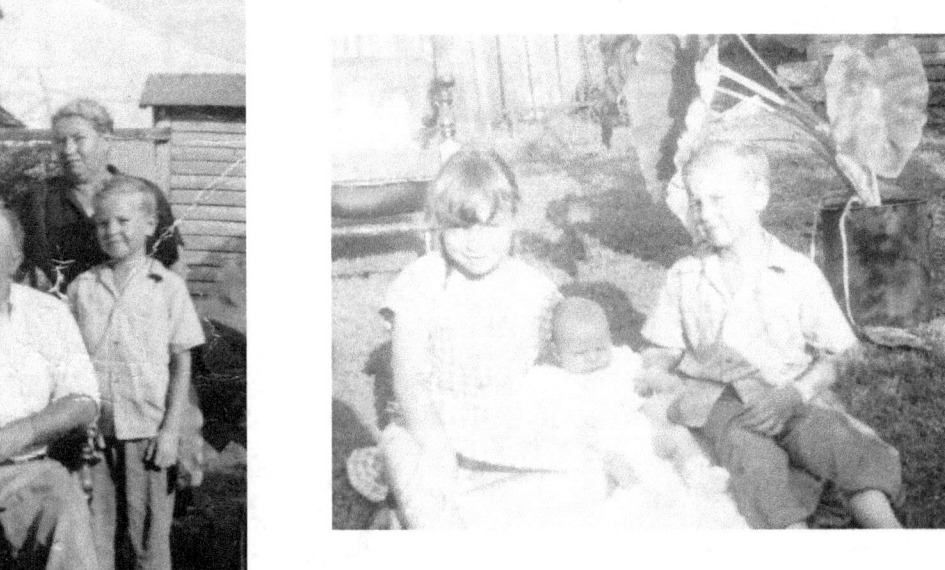

NOTICE OF CLASSIFICATION

Registrant **Paul Padgett,** _____ Order No. **10349**

has been classified in Class _____**3-B**_____ (Until _____ 19___)
by ☒ Local Board   (Insert Date for Class II-A and II-B only)
☐ Board of Appeal (by vote of _____ to _____)
☐ President

_____**Oct. 8 1942**_____, 19_____   *Hoyt L. Lillard*
(Date of mailing)   Member of Local Board.

NOTICE OF RIGHT TO APPEAL

Appeal from classification by local board or board of appeal must be made by signing appeal form on back of questionnaire at office of local board, or by filing written notice of appeal, within ten days after the mailing of this notice.

Before appeal, a registrant may file a written request for appearance within the same ten-day periods and, if he does so, the local board will fix a day and notify him to appear personally before the local board; if this is done, the time to appeal is extended to ten days beyond the day set by the local board for such appearance.

There is a right in certain dependency cases, of appeal from appeal board decision to the President: see Selective Service Regulations.

The law requires you—To keep in touch with your local board. To notify it of any change of address.
To notify it of any fact which might change classification.

D. S. S. Form 57 (Rev. 4-13-41)   16—18071-1   U. S. GOVERNMENT PRINTING OFFICE

Carl Padgett

Son of James and Nancy Padgett

Roy and Zula Padgett

Mary Padgett and Floyd Thomas

 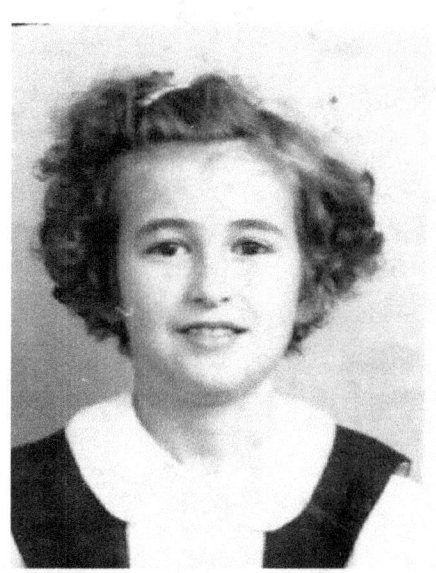

School Days
19   43

Jane Padgett and Toop Lewis

Frank and Nettie McCloud

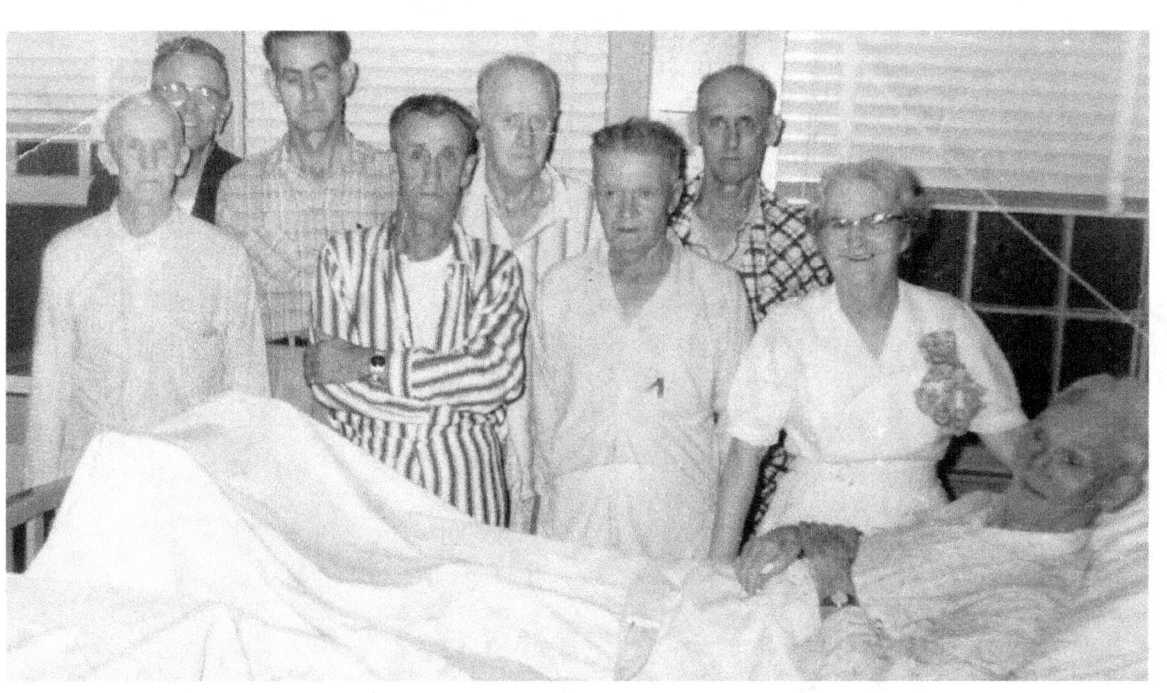

David Sisum

Eunice Padgett's Grandparents

Elisha O. Sisum and Mary Jane Head

Estelle

Lizzie

George

Nelson

Boon

Lizzie Sisum and General Moats

Clarence

Sis

G. W.

Kenneth

Sonny

Audrey "Sis" Moats and Abner Peters

George Washington (G. W.) Moats

Kenneth Moats

Clarence and Ruthie Moats

Sonny and Blanche Moats

Boon and Polly Sisum

Howard Sisum

William Sisum

Regina Sisum

Martha Sisum

Betty Sisum

George Sisum

DELANO SCHOOL   FEB. 1956

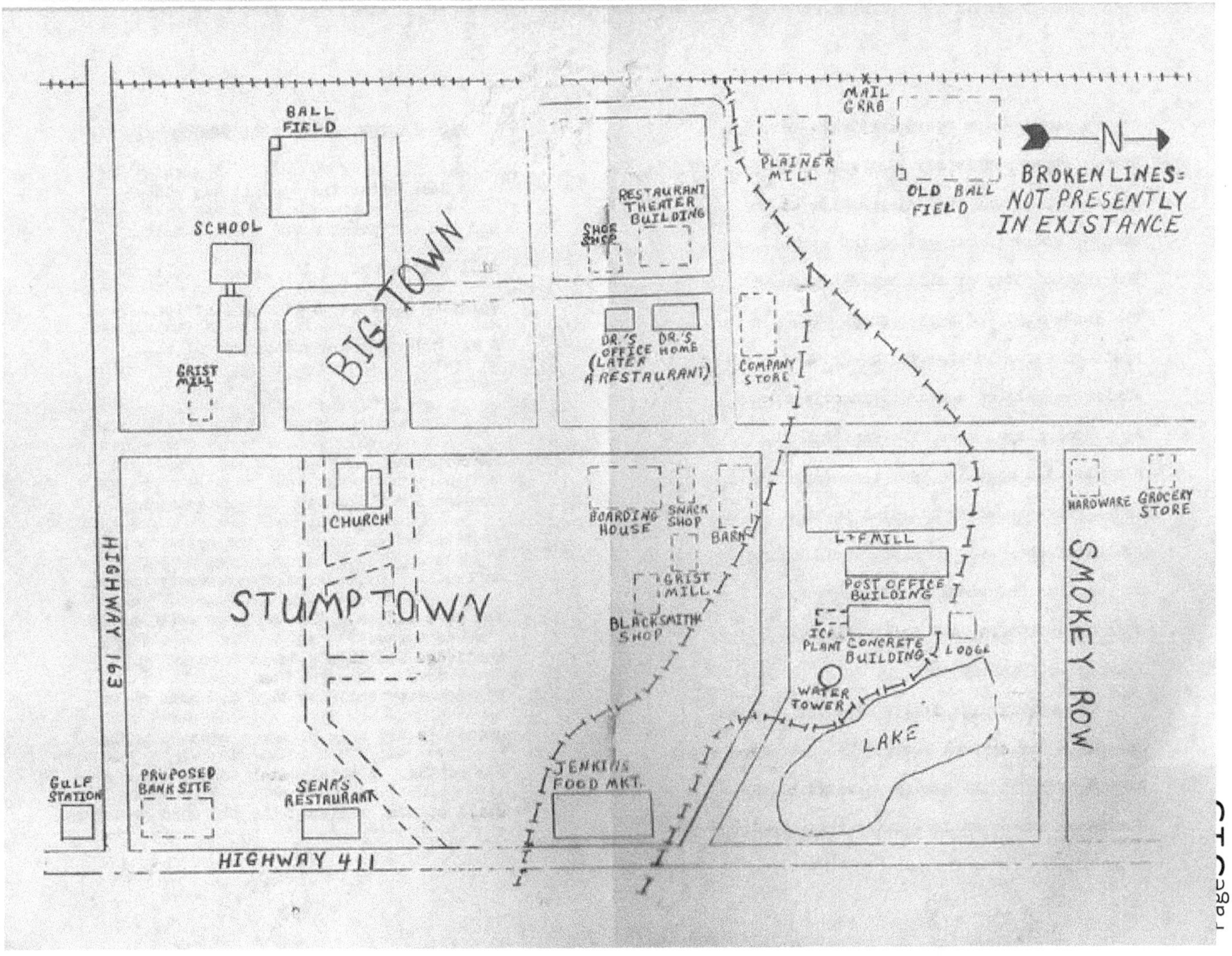

BALL
FIELD

SCHOOL

GRIST
MILL

BIG TOWN

MAIL
GRAB

PLAINER
MILL

OLD BALL
FIELD

N

BROKEN LINES=
NOT PRESENTLY
IN EXISTANCE

RESTAURANT
SHOE
SHOP
THEATER
BUILDING

DR.'S
OFFICE
(LATER
A RESTAURANT)

DR.'S
HOME

COMPANY
STORE

HIGHWAY 163

CHURCH

STUMP TOWN

BOARDING
HOUSE

SNACK
SHOP

BARN

GRIST
MILL

BLACKSMITH
SHOP

L+F MILL

POST OFFICE
BUILDING

ICE
PLANT

CONCRETE
BUILDING

LODGE

HARDWARE

GROCERY
STORE

SMOKEY ROW

WATER
TOWER

LAKE

GULF
STATION

PROPOSED
BANK SITE

SENA'S
RESTAURANT

JENKINS
FOOD MKT.

HIGHWAY 411